# Contacts

In case of an accident, emergency or just advice these are some useful numbers to ring for information and help.

NHS England	tel: 111	www.nhsdirect.nhs.uk
NHS Direct Wales	tel: 0845 4647	www.nhsdirect.wales.nhs.uk
NHS 24 (Scotland)	tel: 08454 24 24 24	www.nhs24.com

Your local Health Visitor can be contacted via your GP practice.

Add your GP's number here

Your local Fire Service can be contacted for advice on fire prevention.

Child Accident Prevention Trust (CAPT) 020 7608 3828
A charity committed to reducing childhood injury.
www.capt.org.uk

**Royal Society for the Prevention of Accidents (RoSPA)
0121 248 2000**
www.rospa.com

Useful numbers in your area:

THE LIVING ROOM

Check all house plants, some may be toxic to your child.

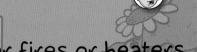

Never hang clothes to dry over fires or heaters, they might fall and catch fire.

Do not overload electrical sockets.

Replace old or worn flexes, they could start a fire.

Always use fireguard for all heaters and fires.

Do not use baby walkers - research shows that they do not teach children to walk, but they can tip over very easily throwing the baby out.

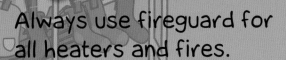

Keep cigarettes and ashtrays out of reach of children.
If you smoke, try not to do it in the same room as children - smoking will damage their health.

Keep hot drinks out of the way of children, hot water can scald 20 minutes after it has boiled.

Keep matches out of reach of children.

Alcohol is toxic to young children, keep it out of reach or in a locked cupboard.

Keep candles out of reach of children and extinguish them completely on leaving a room.

THE KITCHEN

Use door stops to avoid small fingers getting trapped. Remember to remove them and close all doors at night as a fire safety precaution.

Never leave a hot iron unattended. Unplug it immediately after use and put it on a high surface while it cools down. Remember to put the flex and plug out of reach as well.

Avoid using chip pans - a common cause of home fires. Use oven chips or a deep fat frier instead.

Use the back rings when cooking and turn all pan handles away from the edge.

Consider ironing when the kids are in bed.

Don't use the microwave for heating milk or baby food, it can produce dangerous hotspots.

This meat needs to be stored in the fridge. Food should be stored correctly to avoid food poisoning.

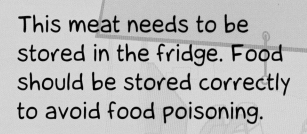

Always strap little ones into high chairs and stay with them whilst they are eating.

Don't leave sharp knives near the edge of the worktop.

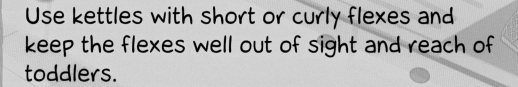

Use kettles with short or curly flexes and keep the flexes well out of sight and reach of toddlers.

Keep plastic bags out of the way to prevent a child from suffocating.

Hall and Stairs

Use rug grips to avoid slipping.

Don't leave toys where they can be tripped over.

Use stair gates for under twos. Make sure that you teach older children how to use the stairs safely.

Make sure that the front / back door cannot be opened by small children, so that they cannot get outside into possible danger. Keep the keys near the door in case of fire, but out of reach of children.

A baby should never be left to feed alone from a propped up bottle as he/she may choke and not be able to push the bottle away.

Throw away damaged or broken toys.

Put safety catches onto windows to stop children from falling out.

Never use duvets or pillows for children under one as they could suffocate.

Keep small toys out of reach of babies and very young children as they could choke on them.

Don't leave anything on the floor that could cause someone to slip or trip.

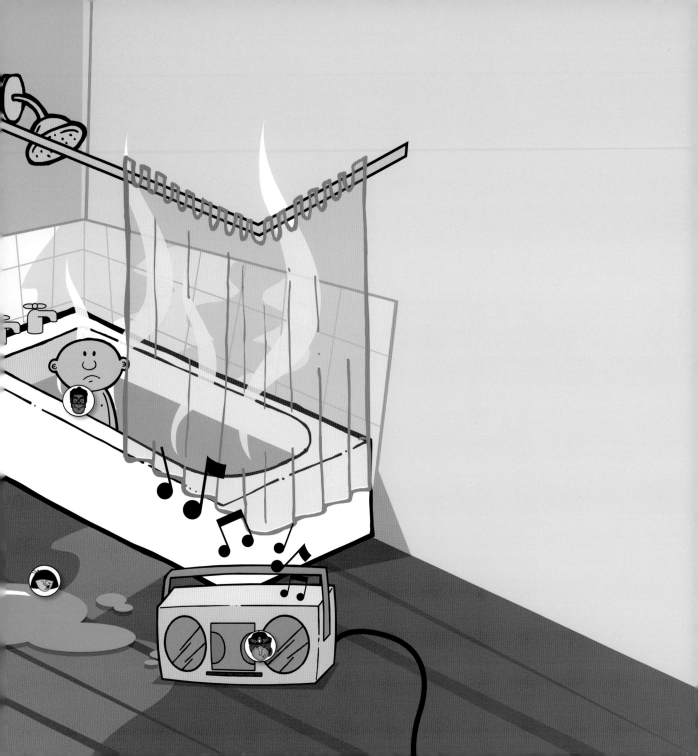

The Bathroom

- Never leave a baby or young child alone in the bath, they can drown in just a few centimetres of water very quickly with no noise or struggle.

- Water from the hot tap can scald. Always run the cold water before the hot and don't leave the hot tap running.

- Electrical appliances should not be used in the bathroom. You could get an electrical shock.

- Keep all cleaning materials out of reach of children.

- Lock medicines in a cabinet or cupboard out of reach of children as they could mistake them for sweets.

  Don't let young children see you taking tablets - they may try to copy you.

- Always put down a mat or towel when bathing or showering to stop the floor becoming a slippery hazard.

Acknowledgments

Both authors feel privileged to have been involved in the pearling industry and to count among their friends so many inspired, innovative and pioneering characters. Special mention must be made of Beverley Kinney, Manager of Deep Water Point pearl farm, and of the indomitable John Fox-Lowe who partnered Bill Reed in pearl farming for many years. Particular thanks are made to Wendy Albert of Kimberley Bookshop, one of the finest bookshops in Australia, for first bringing the two authors together and for her support and encouragement throughout the project. Thanks also to Pat Lowe for casting her sharp editor's eyes over the final manuscript.

Bruce Barker introduced Berni Aquilina to the joys of pearling and diving, while Bruce Farley supported and encouraged her quest to become a pearl-seeding technician. Thanks especially to Rob. Many others – divers, cooks, scientists, shell packers – we salute you all.

Jane Lodge and Emily Rohr have done a splendid job of converting our text and ideas into a book under the artistic direction of Jadwiga Hadrys (Yaja). Without Yaja's tireless endeavours this book would almost certainly not have seen the light of day.

Thanks to friends who modelled jewellery for the photographs:

Jane Autore (inside cover and page 102); Ruby Autore (pages 101, 102 and inside cover); Lucia Galanti (inside cover); Dominika Galecki (inside cover); Elizabeth Guzowski (inside cover); Samantha, Shane and Isaiah Klunder (pages 128-129); Michella Perpignani (pages 114, 115, 122 and inside cover); Renata Schuman (inside cover); Tanya Linney (page 127); Bohdanka Vagner (inside cover, pages 94, 102, 114 and 115); Jarka Vagner (inside cover and page 102). A special thank you to Emily Rohr and Michael Hutchinson who allowed us to use a photograph taken on the occasion of their wedding at Sun Pictures in Broome in 1997 (page 111).

Thanks must also go to Beverley Kinney for allowing access to her collection of books, pictures and ornamental mother–of–pearl.

Lure of the Pearl
Pearl Culture in Australia

Berni Aquilina and William Reed

Designed by Yaja

Kimbooks Publishing Pty Ltd

CONTENTS

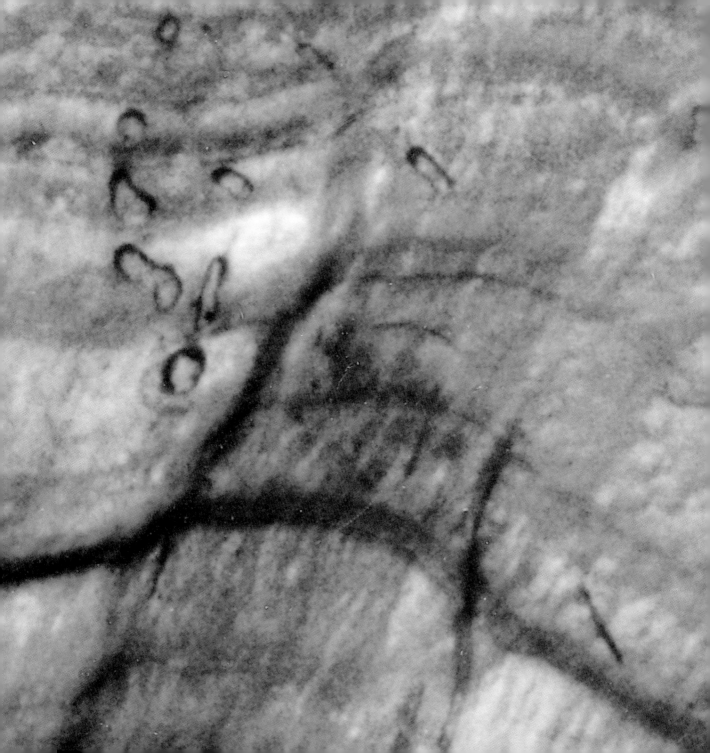

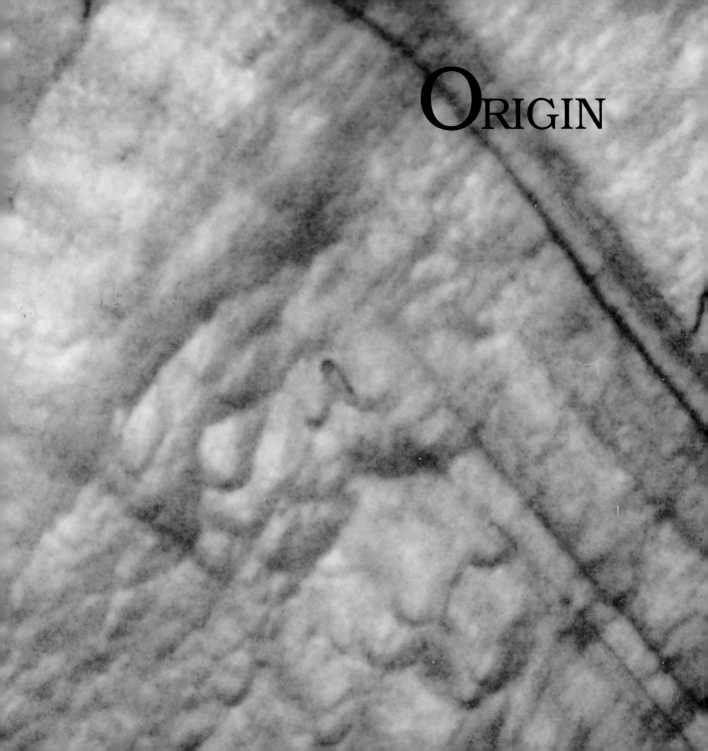

ORIGIN

"the offspring of the shells are pearls that correspond
to the quality of the dew received: if it was a pure inflow,
their brilliance is conspicuous but if it was turbid,
the product also becomes dirty in colour...
If they are well fed in due season, the offspring also grow in size.
If there is lightning, the shells shut up, and diminish in size
in proportion to their abstinence from food;
but if it also thunders they are frightened and shut up suddenly,
producing what are called 'wind-pearls',
which are only inflated with an empty, unsubstantial show:
these are the pearls' miscarriages."

Pliny the Elder, *Natural History, AD 105*

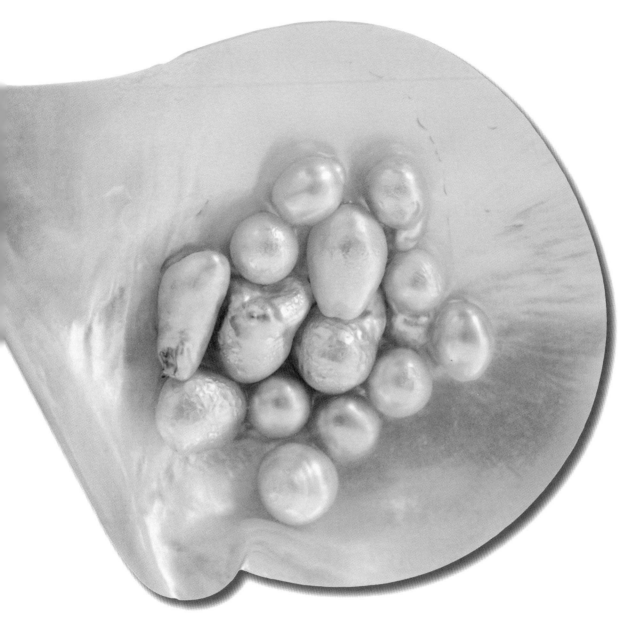

introduction

The soft moon-like gleam of a perfectly formed pearl rarely fails to allure. Pearls have been cherished by almost all the important civilizations on earth. Extensive mythologies developed around them and they became, variously, symbols of purity, wealth, perfection and love.

Most people know that pearls are made by oysters and other shellfish. Children's cartoons depict people diving to the bottom of the sea and finding beautiful pearls cushioned inside giant clams. Anecdotes are told of people biting on a shellfish and finding a pearl. This can happen: a report in the

West Australian, dated 7 November 1995, told of a Western Australian woman who bit on a pearl valued at between $600 and $1,100 while she was eating a jar of chilli mussels. But such serendipity is rare and these stories can be misleading as to the ubiquity and worth of pearls. Natural pearls are so rare that thousands of oysters might have to be opened in order to reveal a single pearl and even then the pearl is likely to be tiny, dark, misshapen and practically worthless. The fact that good quality pearls occur rarely and randomly in

previous page:
The Birth of Venus, 1482, Sandro Botticelli. The Greeks and the Romans associated the birth of Aphrodite or Venus, the goddess of love, with the creation of the pearl

nature has only added to their allure and worth. In the first century A.D. Pliny the Elder wrote that "the first place and the topmost rank among all things of price is held by pearls". Strands of pearls were truly worth a king's ransom, and lay within the province of only the very wealthy.

Pearls are the only gems produced biologically rather than through geophysical processes. Unlike diamonds or other precious stones, pearls don't require cutting or working to reveal their beauty, because they are complete in the form in which they emerge from the oyster. Also, because pearls are formed by the same substances that make the oysters' shells, their appearance is similar to the inside of the shell from which they came. This means that a pearl from the kind of oyster typically served in restaurants will be grey and dull while one from a giant clam will be white like porcelain. Indeed, there are only a few species of oyster that produce the lustrous, iridescent pearls of commercial worth.

Methods for cultivating pearls and for farming pearl oysters were developed early this century, so that pearls could be produced reliably with some control over quality. Cultured pearls are almost identical to natural ones except that a person has activated the process by providing a bead for the pearl to form around. Increased supply of pearls has now reduced their price from that of Pliny's time so that today far more people have the opportunity to own and wear these beautiful gems.

Pearling in Australia began in the mid nineteenth century when extensive new pearling beds of large, thick **mother-of-pearl** shell were discovered off the north-west coast of Australia. The species was named *Pinctada maxima* on account of the shells' size. Soon a booming industry developed, supplying shell throughout the world for use in button-making and inlay work. Following the Second World War and the concomitant development of plastics the demand for mother-of-pearl lessened, to the detriment of the Australian industry. Pearls had never been the mainstay of the mother-of-pearl industry, though as a bonus they were always welcome. However in 1956 the

far left, left & above **pearling in bygone days**

7

first cultured pearl farm in Australia was established with joint Australian, Japanese and American interests. This signalled a new era in Australian pearling as the cultured pearl industry claimed its place as producer of the world's largest pearls. This book briefly describes the workings of the Australian pearling industry as it grows its magnificent white South Sea pearls: how pearl oysters are collected and seeded to grow pearls, how the oysters are cared for while the pearls are growing, and how the pearls are harvested and marketed. It includes some information for buyers of pearls so that they can purchase with confidence and enjoy their choice for many years. Words in bold face are defined in a glossary at the back of the book, where there are also suggestions for further reading. We hope the book answers most of your questions and increases your understanding of a small but valuable Australian industry.

left:
Japanese pearl diver, Etsuzo Kaino wearing full diving suit

below:
diving helmet and boots used until 1975

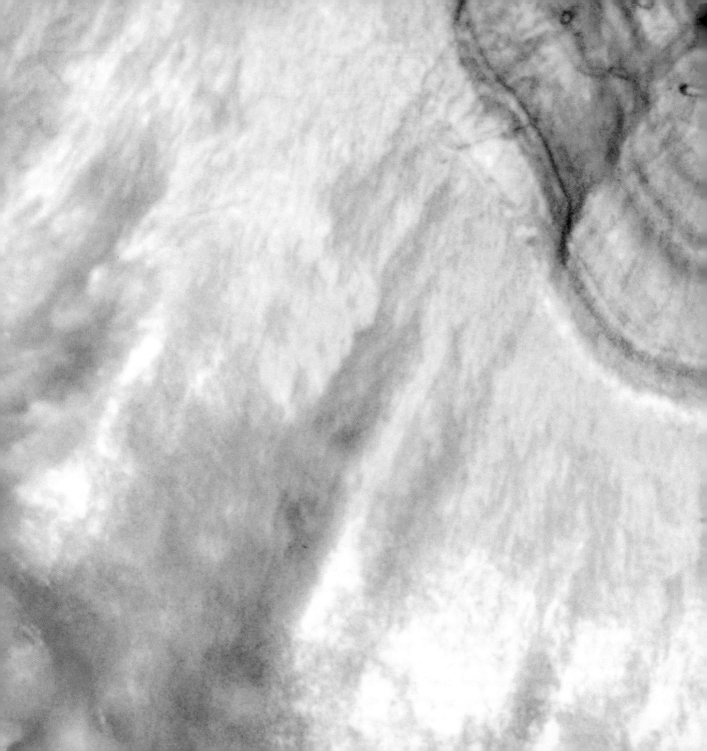

the humble mollusc

Pearls are grown by molluscs, an ancient group of animals that includes oysters, clams and snails. The most important pearl-producing species are from a genus of bivalved molluscs known as pearl oysters. The Australian silver-lipped pearl oyster, Pinctada maxima, *has an appearance and lifestyle that is* typical of the group. To the untrained eye ***Pinctada maxima*** is easy to miss for all its enchanting beauty is contained within the shell. From the outside it is only a dull fawn colour, probably covered with silt and easily mistaken for a rock. It lives a sedentary life on the ocean floor and appears a most

unexciting creature. Yet from these humble and primitive animals come exquisite pearls.

The pearl oyster consists of two half-shells joined by a ligament which forms a hinge. The shell is the skeleton of the animal and the soft, vulnerable parts of the body are enclosed within it. The shell supports the animal's body and at the same time gives it protection. On the outside of a pearl oyster's shell is a thin, horny layer called the prismatic layer. Inside, the shell is lined with a thick coating of pearly **nacre** or mother-of-pearl.

If one of the half-shells is removed, the oyster's **mantle** can be seen. The mantle is a broad, thin and muscular fold of tissue that lies against the shell and secretes the substances that cause the shell to grow. The edge of the mantle is divided into three tiny folds that allow the outside layers of shell to sense light and shadow, and assist muscular action. But the shell's interior layers of nacre are laid down by cells covering the whole outside surface of the mantle that lies against the shell. The mantle plays an important role in pearl production which will be described later.

The diagram opposite shows how the oyster looks under-

Pinctada maxima *opened to reveal the body of the oyster*

previous page:
pearl oyster in natural habitat

neath the mantle. The large kidney-shaped **adductor muscle** controls the opening and closing of the shell. The shell opens when the muscle is relaxed and closes when it contracts.

The oyster feeds and breathes through well-developed gills that hang between the mantle lobes. Pearl oysters feed by siphoning seawater across their gills and by using mucus to trap plankton and particles of detritus from the water. The gills have grooves lined with beating cilia that force the food towards the animal's mouth. Selected food particles are eaten while others are rejected, to be washed away in the water currents. During this process oxygen is also extracted from the seawater that passes across the gills. Other organs in-

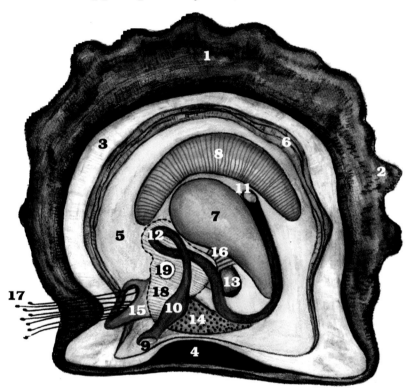

Silver–lipped pearl oyster, *Pinctada maxima*

1. *outer shell (prismatic layer)*
2. *growth finger*
3. *inner shell (nacreous layer)*
4. *hinge*
5. *mantle*
6. *mantle edge, comprising three folds*
7. *adductor muscle*
8. *gills*
9. *mouth*
10. *stomach*
11. *anus*
12. *intestinal loop*
13. *heart*
14. *liver*
15. *foot*
16. *foot retractor muscle*
17. *byssus*
18. *gonad*
19. *position of cultured pearl*

clude a two-chambered heart that pumps colourless blood, a liver and a simple nervous system.

Pearl oysters mature as males but it is possible for them to change sex later. Populations of larger, older oysters are likely to have about a 50:50 ratio of males to females, but this can vary depending on food availability or other environmental conditions. When the oysters are stressed they are less likely to develop as females. Occasionally male and female characteristics are present at the same time in a single oyster.

Silver-lipped pearl oysters spawn during the warm summer months, releasing eggs and sperm into the water. Of the millions of eggs released, only a few survive

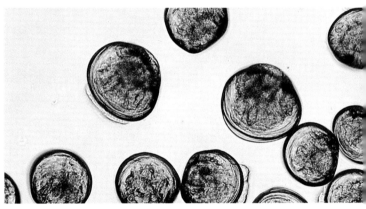

to grow into mature oysters. To do so they must be externally fertilized in the open water, survive a three-week period floating about as larvae in the plankton layer and finally settle on the sea bed. If the young oyster settles on sand it is likely to be abraded to death, while fine mud may smother it. Fortunately the young oyster is able to move about a little with the aid of its muscular foot to find a suitable location. Then it attaches itself to its new home by growing a thread-like tuft, called a **byssus**, which adheres to the pebbles or shell on which it has settled. After about three years the byssus drops away and the pearl oyster remains in place under the weight of its own shell.

As larvae, pearl oysters might be eaten by fish, crabs and other animals, but predators of older pearl oysters must somehow be able to penetrate the oyster's hard shell in order to feast on the soft flesh within. Turtles can crush and break the shell with their strong jaws, starfish and octopus may be able to force open the shell, and some marine snails (such as the murex) can rasp a hole through the shell to gain access. Boring worms and sponges can also destroy the shell, and internal parasites may cause disease.

If the oysters can survive the attacks of predators, including the pearl divers who are paid to collect them, then their natural lifespan is more than ten years. In that time they might grow to a length of 30 centimetres and look as big as a dinnerplate.

Other creatures take advantage of the pearl oyster's protective shell to house themselves safely inside. Small pea crabs are frequent inhabitants of pearl oysters and tiny ghost shrimps are also common. They live near the mouth of the oyster, in the cavity formed by the lobes of the mantle, and feed on particles that are rejected by the oyster.

Silver-lipped pearl oysters are found off the northern Australian coast from Exmouth Gulf in Western Australia to Cairns in Queensland. In Western Australia they have been found from just below the shoreline to a depth of 46 metres. Like most Australians they usually live near the coast, but have been found as far as 46 kilometres offshore. The same species of pearl oyster also grows in tropical waters off Indonesia, Thailand, Burma and the Philippines, but in these locations the oysters are known as gold-lipped pearl oysters because their nacre generally has a yellow border.

*part of the Kimberley coast, a fertile breeding ground for **Pinctada maxima***

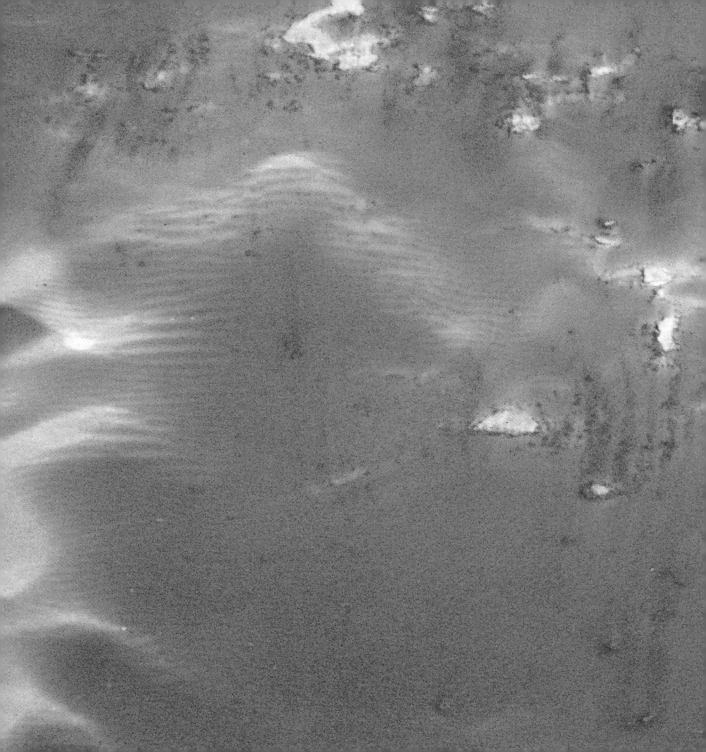

how pearls grow

The ancients believed that pearls were formed from drops of dew or rain and this remained the scientific explanation, at least in Europe, until the 16th century. The Chinese must have known more, because they were cultivating Buddha-shaped images in mussel shells during the 13th century. Shakespeare had an even more romantic notion:

The liquid drops of tears that you have shed,
Shall come again transformed to Orient Pearl...

William Shakespeare, *Richard III*

During the 19th century one popular theory was that pearls originated from the oyster's eggs; another, that they came from

parasites. In fact pearls are simply the result of misplaced nacre-producing mantle cells. The only cells that can produce nacre are those of the outermost skin of the mantle, which lies against the shell. These cells are probably captured inadvertently when some kind of foreign body (such as a small stone, a piece of shell, grain of sand, or even a parasite) penetrates the animal. The cells are able to reproduce themselves and surround the intruding object while the nacre they continue to make coats it, forming a pearl.

The nacre of pearl oysters, whether of shells or pearls, always has the same structure: layer upon layer of microscopic tiles surrounded by a thin membrane that binds them together. The tiles are composed of calcium carbonate crystals in a form called aragonite and are often hexagonal in shape. The membrane, which is called conchiolin or the organic matrix, is made of protein.

In cross-section the layers resemble a brick wall in which the tiles are bricks held together with membrane cement. If a single layer of tiles were seen from above it would look like a mosaic floor, but as the layers are of varying sizes, we always see them overlapping. The surface of nacre, when magnified, looks like a

previous page:
Chinese pearl fishers, French illustrated manuscript of 1338

fingerprint pattern of lines, whorls and spirals formed by the overlapping layers. The components of nacre, both tiles and membrane, are produced by the mantle in a complicated process that scientists do not yet fully understand.

Over the centuries many people have tried to cultivate pearls. The Chinese Buddha images of the 13th century were made from lead or wooden moulds which were inserted between the mussel's shell and the nacre-secreting mantle, then left until they were coated with mother-of-pearl. The Swedish naturalist, Linnaeus, was probably the first European to attempt to grow cultured pearls. In 1761 he inserted small limestone beads attached to fine silver wire inside the valves of mussels.

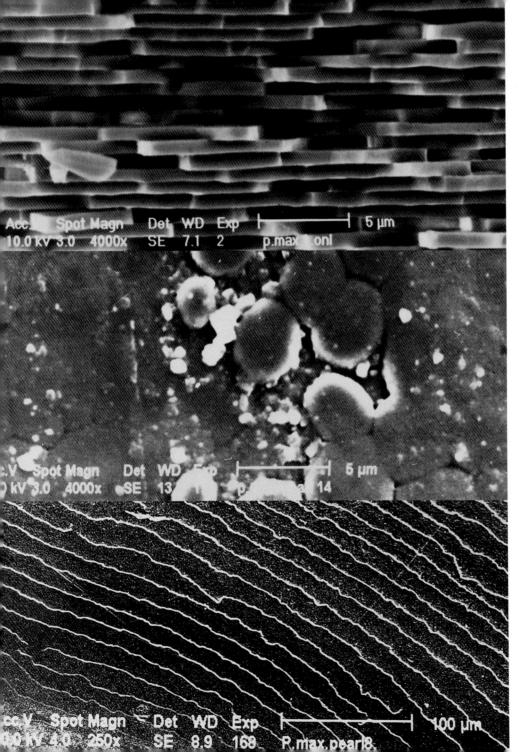

Cross-section of nacre showing its brick-like structure. Notice how all the layers have the same thickness.

The same nacre, but seen from above, showing its mosaic pattern.

The overlapping nacre layers of a pearl showing its fingerprint pattern, visible now at much lower magnification.

The wire kept the balls from coming into contact with the shell. The procedure worked, but the pearls were of low quality.

In Australia a scientist named William Saville-Kent carried out extensive pearl culture experiments during the late 19th century. He made half-pearls by attaching hemispherical beads to the inside of pearl oyster shell in much the same way that the Chinese made their Buddhas. Half-pearls were relatively easy; making **round pearls** was a greater challenge, because the bead cannot be permitted to touch the shell. Saville-Kent did say that he had developed a spherical pearl technique, but he failed to publish the method before his death in 1906.

It was the Japanese who, in a burst of activity early this century, made the breakthrough in the culture of spherical pearls (commonly called cultured or round pearls). In 1904 two people – a scientist named Nishikawa and a carpenter called Mise – almost simultaneously found a successful method. Their technique was to insert surgically a mother-of-pearl bead together with a piece of graft mantle tissue containing nacre-producing cells into a host pearl oyster. After some years of disagreement involving court actions over ownership, a joint patent was eventually issued. The seeding operation commonly used today is based on this technique.

Nishikawa and Mise's stepfather had both visited

Kokichi Mikimoto, credited with developing cultured pearl techniques

Thursday Island, where Saville-Kent was based, in 1901. The similar techniques developed by Mise and Nishikawa and the timing of their discoveries so soon after the Australian visit raises the question of whether or not Nishikawa and Mise (through his step-father) were privy to the results of Saville-Kent's experiments of the previous decade. Did Australia contribute more to cultured pearling than is generally supposed?

Many people know the name Mikimoto. He was the first to sell cultured pearls in Europe. He is also frequently credited with developing cultured pearl techniques. In 1905, after many years of experimentation, Kokichi Mikimoto did succeed in growing a few spherical

pearls. However, his method of completely covering a piece of mother-of-pearl with mantle tissue was a slow and delicate process, resulting in many oyster deaths, and it was soon abandoned. It was Mikimoto's showy and successful approach to business that made his name well known. His greatest victory came after jewellers, with a vested interest in natural pearls that sold for four times the price of Mikimoto's cultured product, tried to prove his pearls false. Following a lawsuit and exhaustive tests, Mikimoto's pearls were declared genuine. David Starr Jordon, a noted biologist and former president of Stanford University in the United States, ruled that natural and cultured pearls

have the same lustre and sheen, a quality which can not be imitated by any form of 'paste' or 'artificial' pearls ... As they are of exactly the same substance and color [sic] as the natural or 'uncultured pearl' there is no real reason why they should not have the same value.

Now most pearls sold are cultured and Australia produces around half a million pearls each year worth some $200 million.

**Australian
South Sea
Pearls**

"We created our own [pearl culture] systems based on our own experience for Australian conditions..."

Nick Paspaley

JOURNEY

fishing shell

The first stage in producing cultured pearls is to find pearl oysters in which the pearls can grow. In Australia pearl oysters, or shell, as the industry calls them, are collected by divers from the wild – especially from the prolific beds off the Eighty Mile Beach, south of Broome. In the old days wooden pearling luggers used to sail out from Broome for months at a time to collect mother-of-pearl, but these days large, comfortable vessels built of steel or fibreglass and equipped with air-conditioning, freezers and modern navigation aids, go to sea for seven to ten days.

Divers are still towed at walking pace about a metre above the sea bed, collecting shell by hand as it comes into view. Formerly one or two divers would have used full diving dress, including brass helmets and heavy lead boots, and breathed air pumped by hand. Modern boats employ four to six divers clad in wet suits, masks and fins, and hydraulic equipment delivers compressed air down through 100 metre hoses.

The diving is done seasonally when wind and weather conditions are likely to

previous page:
**old pearling
lugger**

above:
**modern
pearling
vessel**

right:
**divers
coming up**

*pearlers using
modern diving
equipment*

provide calm seas and good underwater visibility. In Western Australia the diving season extends from February to July. Northern Territory diving is usually carried out in September and October. Extreme tides of up to ten metres occur in northern Australia and during the **springs** the strong tidal currents are dangerous and make visibility poor. Diving takes place during the **neaps** when there is less tidal movement.

The setup for diving is fairly simple. Four or six long ropes, called down-lines, are hung from the boat's **booms**. A 50 kilogram weight is attached to the end of each down-line and lowered almost to the sea floor. Another rope, called the swim-line, is attached to the weight and trails in the

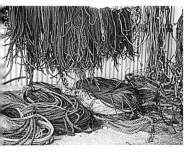

ropes and baskets used in pearl farming

water for 35 metres. The air hoses float behind the boat in a long U-shape, one end connected to the air compressor and the other end, with regulator and mouthpiece, clipped to the diver's weight belt. Each diver descends a down-line and holds onto the swim-line with one hand, using the other to pick up pearl oysters. The divers are able to move backwards and forwards along the swim-line and swing from side to side, but the ropes and air hose always link them to the boat. For safety reasons all divers carry a small tank of air, called a pony bottle or bail-out bottle. This provides a separate air supply to assist their ascent in an emergency.

Young oysters are preferred for culturing pearls because they grow vigorously, are free from parasites, and have a long productive life. It takes two years to grow a pearl, but the same oyster can be used again to grow a second, third, or even fourth pearl. The younger the oyster when first seeded, the more pearls it can grow.

Pearl oysters are usually about 18 months old and perhaps 130 millimetres long, about the size of a saucer, when they are collected. Generally the oysters are not attached to anything and a gentle tug is all that is needed to pick them up. 'Caught' shell are held in a bag made of prawn net that hangs around the diver's neck. When this **neck-bag** is full, the contents are emptied into a larger net bag that is clipped to the down-line. This **big-bag** has a parachute that can be inflated with air from the diver's regulator to raise the heavy shell.

The boat idles along, drifting with the tide across a **patch** of shell-bearing ground. Sometimes a sea anchor, or drogue, is used to further slow it down. The head diver can communicate with the boat using a signal system, similar to Morse-code, to control the speed and direction of the vessel.

Silver-lipped pearl oysters are usually found on a **garden bottom** where colourful sponges, corals and seaweeds are growing. Sometimes they are found in **potato country** where numerous sea-squirts are scattered over a firm sandy bottom. It is rare to find silver-lipped pearl oysters on bare sand or rock. In recent years improved echo sounders have allowed the boat captain to determine the type of sea floor he is travelling over without constantly needing to send a diver down to test the bottom. Even more importantly, the development of the Global Positioning System (GPS) and radar now means that the vessel's position can be

turning panels on the garden bottom

*coming up at
the end of
a drift*

precisely recorded, making it easy for the captain to return to a good patch in future years. Catch rates increased dramatically a few years ago, and GPS has been credited as the most likely reason for it.

At the end of the patch the divers ascend to the surface with their shell.

'The bends' is an affliction that used to be suffered by mother-of-pearl divers early this century and often led to loss of life. It is a type of decompression sickness caused by nitrogen bubbles forming in the bloodstream or body tissues following too rapid an ascent. Breathing oxygen assists the body to get rid of excess nitrogen, so divers working in deep water stop on ascent at a depth of six to nine metres and swap their regulator, through which they have been breathing compressed air, for another that supplies medical oxygen from storage bottles on the ship's deck. After breathing oxygen for a prescribed time the divers can finally finish their ascent and have a brief rest or a hasty meal on board the vessel while it returns to the start of the patch to begin the next **drift**.

The same area can be worked over several times until the catch rates are too poor to be worthwhile. The diving routine begins at first light and continues until dark with each drift lasting about 45 minutes. Divers are paid according to the number of pearl oysters they collect, so there is always fierce competition as to which diver will catch the most shell.

Once on deck, the live pearl oysters are sorted. Any large, old or otherwise unsuitable shell are returned to the sea bed to breed. The others are counted then scrubbed and cleaned to remove encrusting algae and other growth before being placed in wire-framed netting panels, each holding six oysters in pockets that are tied shut to prevent accidental losses. The panels, which protect the oysters from predators and are numbered for accounting purposes, are attached to long ropes, called **longlines,** and lowered again to the sea bed in selected holding areas. The oysters are left on these **dumps** until the operating season begins.

oyster shells covered in algae and other organisms

Diving sounds romantic but in fact it is extremely hard, and often dangerous, work. The underwater visibility is sometimes only a metre or so and even on the best days it is seldom more than five metres. One diver aptly described his work as being "like collecting mushrooms in a fog". The poor visibility can make divers nervous, too, of what they might encounter without warning. Divers often see sea snakes, large cod, turtles, sharks and rays. In 1993 an unfortunate diver on a pearl farm lost his life when a tiger shark ripped him from his diving gear. This was the first recorded killing of a Western Australian pearl diver by a shark in modern times.

oysters in netting panels

The wild pearl oyster catch is strictly controlled by the State Fisheries Departments who allocate **quotas** for each pearling licence issued. Quotas serve to protect wild oyster stocks from over exploitation, but they also keep pearl prices high by regulating the number of pearls produced. Quotas are reviewed by monitoring the number of oysters collected per hour and the number of hours spent diving for them.

To protect juvenile stocks the Western Australian Fisheries Department also sets a minimum size, at present 120 millimetres, for oysters that can be taken by divers. The total live pearl shell quota for the Broome area is now about 500,000 oysters annually, with a further 115,000 shell allocated for Western Australia's southern pearling area between Port Hedland and Exmouth Gulf. Paspaley Pearling Company, Australia's largest pearl producer, fished over 300,000 oysters last year; several small companies each fished 15,000 shell. The Northern Territory has a fishing quota of 120,000 pearl oysters each year, which may be taken live or killed for mother-of-pearl. Queensland's small pearling industry is not subject to quotas.

hatching oysters

Few countries can cultivate their pearls in oysters caught from the wild as Australia can. In Japan, pollution has reduced natural oyster populations, and nearly all Japanese oysters begin life in land-based hatcheries. Indonesia also depends on artificially bred pearl oysters because the few wild ones that they have live in deep water and collecting them is hazardous. Australia is lucky to have a long unpolluted coastline and the valuable resource of the Eighty Mile Beach fishing ground where most of Australia's wild oysters are collected. Nevertheless hatcheries have been under consideration

in Australia, because catching oysters in the wild is an expensive business. It is estimated that $25 is spent on running boats and employing divers for each pearl oyster collected. There is also a risk of some disaster destroying natural stocks. Cyclones have been known to denude pearling beds, and recovery can take many years. However, hatcheries require at least an 18 month investment of time and energy while the oysters are grown to a useful size.

In 1983 the Western Australian Fisheries Department began research to propagate silver-lipped oysters artificially. The research was successfully completed in 1990 and a commercial hatchery opened soon afterwards. Mature oysters, called broodstock, can be made to spawn in laboratory tanks by immersing them in ultraviolet irradiated seawater, manipulating temperature and adding ripe eggs and sperm to the water.

seventeen day old pedi-veliger larva showing foot

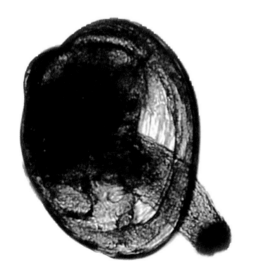

Larval oysters are fed microalgae grown for the purpose, and surfaces are provided for the developing oysters to settle on. When the young oysters, called **spat**, are about six millimetres long they are carefully removed to a sea-based **grow-out** area. Housed in protective mesh to keep predators away, the spat are regularly cleaned to promote

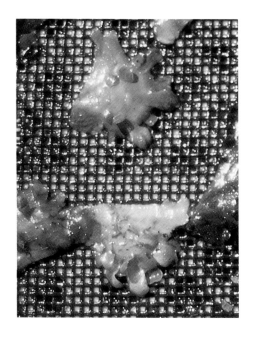

growth. As they increase in size, densities are reduced to ensure they are well fed. When they reach about 90 millimetres in length the young oysters, by now called **chicken shell**, are transferred to bigger panels ready for seeding.

Strict protocols for the movement of oysters have been developed by the Fisheries Department and the pearling industry to control the spread of parasites and disease. Spat cannot leave the hatchery without a clean bill of health. Further, they must be quarantined in the grow-out area and receive a second health check before they can be put near other pearl oysters. Occasionally an entire shipment of thousands of spat can fail the

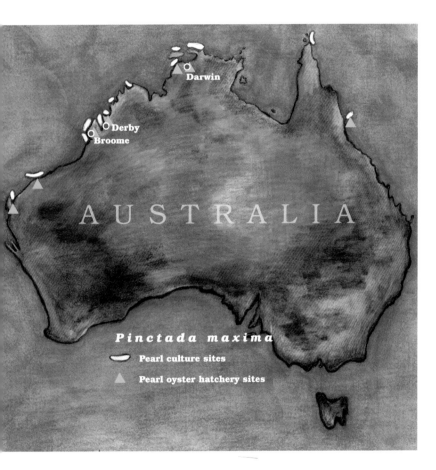

Pinctada maxima

◡ Pearl culture sites

▲ Pearl oyster hatchery sites

health test and must be destroyed.

Five years ago industry resistance to hatchery production in Australia was very strong, mainly due to fears that over-production of oysters would reduce the price of pearls. Spat grow-out had also proved difficult, and there were doubts that hatcheries could be commercially viable. However, attitudes are changing and Australia now has several hatcheries. Hatchery production, like the wild oyster take, is controlled by a quota system. The Northern Territory, which expects its future pearling industry to be based on hatchery produced rather than fished pearl oysters, has a total hatchery quota of 300,000 oysters. In Western Australia the Fisheries Department has issued options of 20,000 hatchery oysters to each of its pearl culture licence holders for trial periods of ten to thirteen years. The options will be converted to quotas if they are being successfully exploited at the end of the time.

Spat collection is commonly used in other countries as another way to get oysters without diving for them. Prawn net or shade-cloth is hung in the water early in summer when spawning is likely to take place. Spat settling on these collectors can be left to grow to about 1 cm in size before being moved into mesh panels for on-growing. Spat collection is a time-consuming process because many other species that look similar at a young age also settle on the collectors and separating

them can be difficult. In Australia only one pearling company has seriously attempted spat collection, with mixed results.

spat holder ready to go on line.

spat inside cages.

spat

seeding the pearl

The first seeding operation, in which the technician surgically inserts a bead nucleus and mantle graft into a pearl oyster to make a pearl grow is the single most important step in the cycle of pearl culture. Oysters can die from the stress of the operation and from exposure to wind and cold while they are out of the water. As well, the skill of the **technician** is correlated with the quality of the pearl harvested two years later on. Recently, much attention has been paid to improving the conditions of this operation. Pearl seeding used to be done on open rafts that exposed the oysters

to drying winds and lacked the facilities of lights and running water. Today **seeding** operations are conducted aboard modern, comfortable vessels that contain large tanks through which seawater can be pumped, and which hold the live oysters until their operation. The operating season runs from about May to September when water temperatures are low and the oyster's reproductive organ, called the **gonad**, is not developed. This is important because the implant is placed in the same place that the gonad develops and the operation cannot be performed when the gonad is ripe.

Three things are essential for a pearl seeding operation: a **nucleus**, a pearl oyster, and a piece of mantle tissue to use as a **graft**. Nuclei are manufactured by tumbling and polishing cubes of mussel or clam shell until they are spherical. Mussel shells from the Mississippi River are preferred because they can be drilled without cracking, they expand and contract at the same rate as the nacre that will coat them, and because they are thick enough to produce the largest nuclei used: 15 millimetres in diameter. A day's supply of oysters, which have been fished earlier in the year, is kept in the ship's tanks. The technician kills

some of these to provide the mantle tissue used in the seeding operation. He prepares the graft pieces by first removing the outer edge of the mantle because it produces the horny brown outer parts of shell instead of nacre. Then the rest of the mantle containing the nacre-producing epithelial cells is carefully cut into small pieces each about the size of a match head. One animal can produce about fifty tissue grafts.

preparation of graft tissue:

1. shell with mantle intact

2. shell after mantle has been cut away

3. strips of mantle tissue from which small graft pieces are prepared

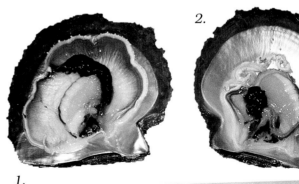

1.

2.

3.

Clean oysters are carefully opened by deckworkers using a special tool, wedged to keep the two halves of the shell from closing again, placed in trays each holding about 20 oysters, and passed to the technician. To perform the seeding operation the technician removes the wedge, replacing it with special pliers that permit access to the operation area. The gills, which hang in the space between the mantle lobes, are gently separated to expose the body of the oyster. The thread-like byssus is severed if it is putting tension on the operation area. Pea crabs or shrimps living in the mantle cavity may also be moved out of the way. Now a passage is cut from the foot of the oyster to its gonad into which a nucleus and piece of

cleaned oysters ready to be seeded

mantle tissue are inserted. Care is taken that the nacre-secreting cells on the outside of the mantle piece are lying against the nucleus, otherwise the nacre will not coat the bead. Nuclei used in this initial seeding operation are between six and eleven millimetres in diameter; larger ones are used in later years. Tools resembling dentists' instruments are used to perform the operation.

tools used for the seeding operation

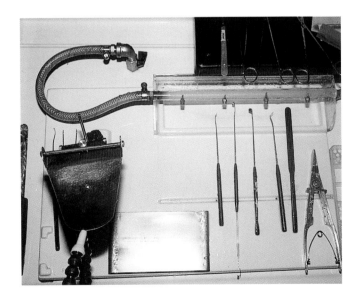

Seeded oysters are returned to the net panels and attached to longlines anchored to the sea bed. If the operation is successful the nacre-producing cells of the mantle piece will reproduce, graft onto the oyster's body tissue, and eventually form a pearl sac around the nucleus.

The **pearl sac** secretes layers of nacre that coat the nucleus, forming a pearl. To help the pearl sac form evenly around the nucleus, divers turn the panels of oysters from one side to the other every few days for about six weeks. After this **turning program** the oysters are left on the bottom until it is convenient to move them to the pearl farm. The farms are usually hundreds of kilometres from the fishing grounds where the oysters are seeded. In the case of Paspaley Pearling Company, wild oysters are caught and seeded at Eighty Mile Beach before being moved to the company's pearl farms at the Cobourg Peninsula in the Northern Territory, a distance of 1,500 kilometres. The trip by boat takes four days. The oysters travel in shell tanks on board the vessel. Seawater is pumped through these tanks continuously during the trip.

Even though the seeding operation seems simple it requires skill, dedication and a steady hand. An experienced technician working under ideal conditions can seed up to six hundred oysters a day, out of which 80 percent might successfully grow pearls. A trainee will probably seed only two hund-

**oysters
wedged
open**

*previous
page:*
**Deep Water
Point pearl
farm**

red shell in a day and could be disappointed by a success rate as low as 30 percent. Success is measured by the percentage of operated oysters that survive the operation and the percentage of these that grow nucleated pearls. Failure can result if the nucleus is expelled from the oyster's body, if the cells of the mantle piece die, or if the mantle piece is not correctly aligned with the nucleus.

Many oysters can die at the hands of an inexperienced technician, and the pearls that are grown in the others might be of low quality. With oysters costing about $25 each and pearls worth an average of $300, the training of new technicians becomes a costly proposition. For this reason experienced technicians are in great demand, and their skills can command high remuneration.

Seeding technicians come mostly from Japan, although many are now permanent residents or citizens of Australia. There is also a slowly increasing number of qualified and competent Australian technicians. Of about 60 pearl technicians presently working in Australia more than 40 are of Japanese descent; fifteen years ago all but one were Japanese. In 1922, in a misguided attempt to protect the natural pearl industry, the Western Australian government prohibited any work or experimentation on the cultivation of pearls. The law was not repealed until 1949, by which time the Japanese had their pearling technology well developed and were in a position to give technical assistance and financial backing when Australia's first pearl farm began work in 1956. That farm, named Kuri Bay after one of its founders, Mr Kuribayashi, is situated about 350 kilometres north of Broome and can only be approached by sea or air. At the time it was thought unreasonable for Australians of European descent to work in such a remote location; for many years Japanese technicians and Thursday Islander labourers worked at Kuri Bay for up to 12 months at a time. Now most of the technicians work at Australian pearl farms for only the brief seeding season, and may do similar work overseas in Tahiti, Indonesia and elsewhere at other times of the year.

left:
technician Koiso seeding a shell

below:
pearl oysters after seeding

the pearl farm

*Pearl farming methods vary between companies and according to the location. The most common system used in Australia today involves suspending pearl oysters, held in netting panels, from **dropper-lines** attached to massive longlines. The 24 to 28 millimetre diameter longlines are buoyed by* numerous plastic floats and held in place with large steel or cement anchors. The oysters hang a few metres beneath the surface where maximum food is available. Strong currents and fierce monsoon storms make such expensive systems necessary to protect the valuable, seeded pearl oysters.

Visitors to pearl farms only see row after row of floats on the surface of the water and are amazed by the seeming lack of action. However, below the surface the primitive mollusc in its watery workshop is busily laying down coat upon coat of iridescent nacre. In two or three years this may become a priceless gem. Scientists, in modern laboratories with vast resources, have not yet succeeded in imitating the artistry of this humble mollusc!

Farm sites are usually situated in fertile waters with

good tidal currents so that food is abundant and replenished every day. Unfortunately, fertile water also harbours many fouling organisms, such as barnacles, sea-squirts and seaweeds. They attach to the longlines, panels and shell, weighing them down and sometimes causing longlines to sink or break. Most animal foulers are filter-feeders like the pearl oysters and are competing for the same food, to the detriment of the pearl oyster and its growing pearl. Regular cleaning of lines and shell to control fouling is therefore essential.

Shell cleaning is done on custom-built aluminium workboats six to ten metres long. The panels and their oysters, still tied by droppers to the longline, are hauled up and fed through a clean-

previous page:
longlines in a protected bay

panels containing oysters ready to be cleaned

70

ing machine in a manner that resembles a car going through an automatic carwash. High pressure water hits the panels of oysters from top and bottom. This is generally enough to dislodge seaweed, but encrusting oysters, barnacles and sea squirts must be removed by hand when the panels emerge from the machine.

Most pearl farms clean their oysters at least monthly; in some places and at certain times of the year it is necessary to clean every second week. Shell cleaning is a dirty, monotonous job that produces a high turnover of workers. Even so, some people enjoy the lifestyle of working on the water in some of the most remote and magnificent parts of Australia, and stay for years.

machine in operation

cleaned oysters

Unlike earlier times when people spent months on end at the farm, today workers are likely to alternate between a fortnight at the pearl farm and a week in town.

Some months after the initial seeding operation the operated oysters are x-rayed to determine whether a pearl has begun to form. Those that are not growing a cultured pearl, either because they have rejected the nucleus or because the graft tissue was not in proper contact with it, are put aside for another operation attempt. X-raying the oysters is a way to ensure that money is not being spent on shell not growing a pearl.

Pearling is a risky business and definitely not for the

diver cleaning pearl oyster shells

faint-hearted. Natural hazards include cyclones and disease that can wipe out a crop of oysters. Economic risk comes from the high costs of maintaining boats and equipment, and paying salaries. As pearls are luxury items their price is closely linked to world economic cycles and has been known to drop by half during a depression.

Usually the time of greatest risk for a pearl farmer is during the first years when capital expenditure is high, cultivation systems are still being developed, and harvests have not begun to bring in regular income. But even well-established farms can fail. 'Shock closure of pearl farm ... The world's biggest pearl farm at Kuri Bay ... is to close', read the headlines of the Weekend News in July 1983. A company official said the closure was a 'commercial decision' that had been forced by a series of problems including a cyclone that had hit the farm four months before and killed large numbers of oysters, rising numbers of oyster deaths from a 'mysterious disease', soaring costs, and a 45 percent drop in the price of pearls. In fact the farm continued to operate at a reduced level for a few more years until it was sold to Paspaley Pearling Company in 1989.

This 'mysterious disease' ravaged pearl farms in the late 1970s and early 1980s. Kuri Bay was reported to be losing more than 50 percent of its oysters and other farms were reporting death rates of 20 percent. Scientific researchers later attributed

the deaths to poor handling that allowed bacteria, normally present in seawater, to build up to dangerous levels. New handling systems were devised and death rates were reduced. Some of the improvements included reducing stocking densities, seeding the oysters at the fishing grounds instead of at farms, changing transportation schedules to suit natural temperature cycles, paying greater attention to hygiene during operation, and reducing transport times. Now death rates on the farms are usually only a few percent per year.

Deep Water Point pearl farm and its colours

the harvest

Harvest time occurs after the pearl oysters have been carefully nurtured for two years. It is a time of anticipation and heightened spirits: everyone hopes for a good crop. Usually a boat comes to the pearl farm and all the harvesting is done aboard. As before, the oysters are moved to a holding tank on board and wedged open. However the technician doesn't need to prepare mantle grafts because the oyster already has a reusable pearl sac that is growing around the pearl to be harvested. X-rays have ensured that almost all the oysters being harvested contain a pearl, although the pearl's

quality is not known. It is not necessary to kill the oyster in order to retrieve its pearl; the technician can surgically remove the pearl, cutting into the pearl sac and hooking the pearl out. If the pearl is of good quality and the oyster is healthy, a second nucleus, almost as large as the pearl that was removed, can be placed in the empty pearl sac. Two years later this second pearl will be harvested and the process repeated a third, and even fourth, time. If at any harvest the oyster is unhealthy or grows a poor

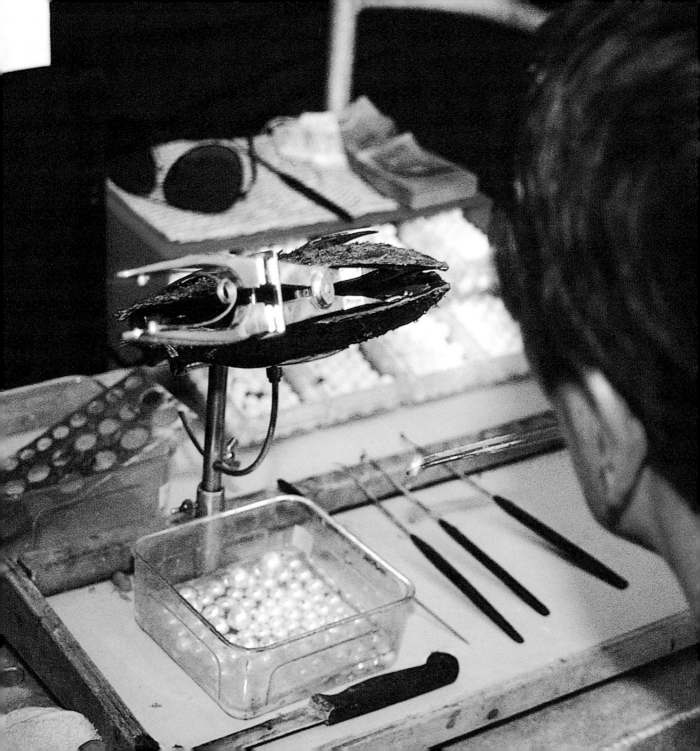

pearl then it will be killed or used to grow half pearls, as described later. At the first pearl harvest two thirds of the oysters might be reseeded but at future harvests, when the oysters are older and less healthy, half of them might be culled.

Sometimes bright, tiny pearls are found. These *keshi*, or seed pearls, grow from a graft mantle piece inserted at the time of the first operation, that is not in contact with a nucleus. It still makes a tiny pearl sac and secretes nacre to form a pearl without a nucleus, almost identical to a natural one.

At the end of a harvesting day the pearl farmer may have collected a bucket of pearls. They are cleaned to remove mucus, then rinsed in clean, fresh water and dried. Now the farmer and technicians have the opportunity to study and discuss the crop. Pearls can be misshapen, discoloured or have dull, pitted surfaces and be worth only a few dollars each, or they might be perfect, large, round gems each worth more than $10,000. It is very exciting to harvest a rare and perfect gem, but what really counts for the

left:
harvesting the pearls

below:
sorting the harvest

*Penny
Arrow
and
Serena
Sanders
(above) as
well as
Justine
Kinney
(right)
delighted
with the
harvest*

pearl farmer is the average price of all the pearls produced compared with the amount that was spent growing them. A novice seeing a rare gem may think it will bring an enormous profit: cost of oyster $25; look after it for two years and sell the pearl for $5,000. But this formula cannot be extrapolated over the whole crop. The majority of pearls are worth hundreds, not thousands, of dollars and their value must be offset against the costs of running boats and farms, paying crews, and the risks of natural disasters wiping out the crop.

Silver–lipped pearl oysters will usually lay down at least a millimetre of nacre over the nucleus each year. This means that a nucleus six millimetres in diameter will produce a ten millimetre pearl after two years. If the oyster is re-seeded with a nine millimeter nucleus the second pearl harvested might be 13 millimetres in diameter. Further operations will continue to make bigger pearls. However, as the oysters become older growth rates slow, health declines as parasites invade the shells, and the quality of the pearls diminishes.

Half pearls, also called *mabe* or blister pearls, are made by peeling back the mantle to expose the inside of the oyster's shell and gluing flat-based plastic beads onto each half of the shell. The beads are usually dome-shaped but sometimes other shapes such as tear-drops or hearts are used. Typically, seven half pearl nuclei can be placed in each oyster. As the inside of the shell coats with nacre, so do the beads, and the half pearl caps can be harvested about nine months after the operation. Because the half pearls are incorporated into the shell they can only be removed by drilling with a hole-saw, and for this the oyster must be killed. The half pearl operation is a simple one because no surgery is required on the oyster's body, and a novice technician can learn the procedure in a day or two. 'Round pearl' technicians who seed and harvest full pearls are usually not interested in working with half pearls so farmworkers and other people often get the job.

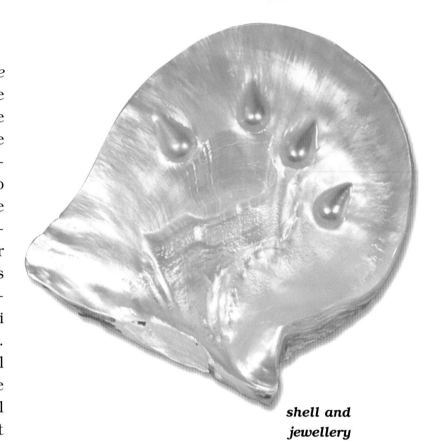

shell and jewellery with mabe pearls.

*pearl
meat
drying*

right:
**packing
mother-of-
pearl (MOP)**

opposite:
**mother-of-
pearl
bric-a-brac
and pearl
meat dish**

When oysters are killed the pearl shell meat – which is actually the adductor muscle which controls the opening and closing of the shell – is removed carefully. It is a valuable by-product, dried and exported to Asian markets or frozen for use in local restaurants. The fresh meat has a fibrous texture and delicious flavour, similar to abalone. Some people believe it to be an aphrodisiac.

The shells from killed oysters are another valuable by-product worth up to ten thousand dollars a tonne, depending on quality. Pearl shell is sold to European button manufacturers and to Asian markets for carving and inlay work. Guitar and banjo fingerboards are commonly inlaid with mother-of-pearl.

grading

There is no point in growing pearls if they cannot be sold for a good price and to do this successfully the farmer must understand the market. Selling the cream of the crop for a high price may seem inviting, but not if it means the farmer is left with a gemless bag of low quality pearls that no-one will buy at any price. To achieve the best price for a crop all the pearls must be carefully valued taking into account the whole range of qualities that will be present in one harvest. Then an average price accurately reflecting the value of the crop can be set. The pearls must first be divided into groups

that are closely matched for characteristics of size, shape, colour, lustre, and flaws. This process is called **grading.**

Before grading begins, the pearls are lightly polished to remove any residue of mucus. Unlike the bleaching and dying processes that Japanese pearls are subject to, this light polish is the only treatment Australian pearls receive.

Shape and size are the easiest characteristics to grade for. Even though cultured pearls are often called 'round

*grading
pearls
according
to their
size,
shape,
colour and
lustre*

pearls' only about 20 percent of them are likely to be
spherical. Most of the other
pearls will still be symmetrical along one axis and
shaped like pears, called
drops, or buttons. The few
that are not symmetrical are
called baroque or semi-
baroque, depending on how
irregular their shape is.
Non-round pearls are formed when pressure from muscle or other hard tissue
deforms the pearl's shape.
Sometimes parallel grooves
are etched in rings around
the pearl, producing what
are called circle or ring
pearls.

While the pearls are being
sorted into their shapes,
completely unsaleable pearls
are removed, to be either
destroyed or ground back
into nuclei. Unsaleable
pearls look ugly and are

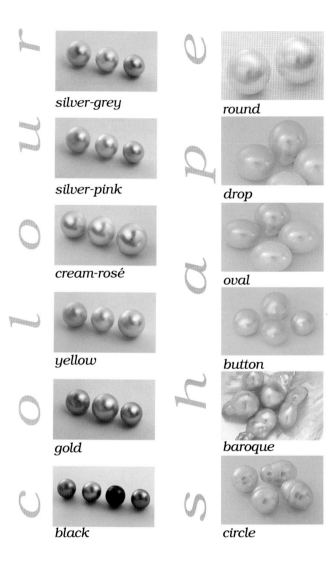

colour

silver-grey

silver-pink

cream-rosé

yellow

gold

black

shape

round

drop

oval

button

baroque

circle

marked by holes, dark stains from organic deposits, or have a dull surface. Tiny keshi pearls are also removed, to be sold separately. After sorting, each shape category is sieved into sizes ranging from 10 to 18 millimetres in diameter. (Pearls are always measured by the length of their shortest axis).

Pearls from silver–lipped pearl oysters are usually silver-white, but they also come in shades of yellow, cream and blue-grey. Chemicals in the organic part of the nacre are responsible for the cream and yellow shades, while the darker blue-grey tones are caused by anomalous deposits of dark coloured organic material around the nucleus. Even though a nucleus may be coated with several milli-

91

metres of nacre, some light still penetrates these layers and can be reflected from material surrounding it.

Apart from these base colours, pearls often show beautiful iridescent overtones, especially pinks and greens. These colours arise from the layered structure of nacre and the behaviour of light as it reflects from both the upper and lower surfaces of these layers. At certain thicknesses of layer the light reflected from the lower surface will be in phase with light reflected from the upper surface, producing interference patterns that cause iridescence. The effect normally occurs in structures with thicknesses in the range of the wavelengths of visible light, that is between 0.4 and 0.7 micrometres. Nacre tiles, which are be-

tween 0.3 to 0.5 micrometres thick, fall into this range.

Lustre, that captivating quality of shining radiance, is the most important characteristic of a gem quality pearl. Lustre is closely related to iridescence: both are due to the interaction between nacre structure and the behaviour of light. The best lustre occurs when the crystal tiles in nacre are deposited in parallel, even layers. Poor lustre happens when the tiles are deposited unevenly or when crystals of different size are growing together.

The more heavily a pearl is flawed the lower its price will be. Pitting of the pearl's surface is a common flaw that probably occurs when some of the cells of the pearl sac are damaged and unable to produce nacre, or if specks of foreign matter become trapped between the pearl sac and the pearl. Stains, like blue pearls, are the result of organic material being deposited on parts of the pearl's surface. Scratch-marks are occasionally made by the knife of a careless technician.

Thin coatings of nacre will also reduce the price of pearls because lustre and colour are affected. In extreme cases, thin coats of nacre will crack and split. This has become a problem with some Japanese cultured pearls, when they are cultured for less than a year and have coatings as thin as 0.1 millimetre. To last a lifetime a pearl needs to have a coating of at least 0.4 millimetres. This is no problem for Australia: the nacre coat-

ing Australian pearls is more than two millimetres thick, enough to last several lifetimes.

When all the pearls have been sorted, each category is weighed and the average weight of the pearls is calculated. The traditional weight measure used is the Japanese *momme* which is equal to 3.75 grams. A 13 millimetre pearl weighs about one *momme.*

Usually a grader will make some attempt to match pearls, because matched pearls can fetch a higher price. Pearls are paired for earrings and are made into strands of 30 or more matching pearls for necklaces. Matching the pearls is a painstaking task because although each pearl is unique, a companion must

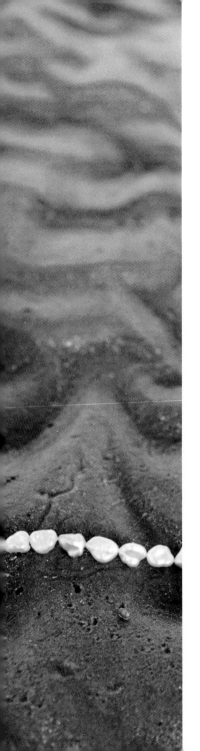

be sought with all the same qualities of size, shape, colour, lustre. Necklace pearls are usually drilled and made into temporary strands, which do not attract the same rate of export duty as finished items of jewellery. The drill is a special tool that uses two bits and drills from both sides at once. The drill sites are carefully selected to obscure as many flaws as possible.

Now is the exacting but crucial time of setting the price for each grade of pearls: all the criteria used to grade the pearls are taken into account in reaching this decision. Prices of pearls follow market demand. Perfect round or perfect drop shaped pearls with a silver-pink colour are the most costly. Deep gold colours and silver or silver-grey are also very valuable. Yellow pearls are worth only half the value of silver-white ones. Pearls with very high lustre command high prices, as do those more than 15 millimetres in size. Ultimately, however, the right price is the one that customers are prepared to pay.

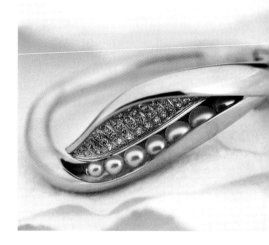

jewellery from the Linneys of Broome & Subiaco collection

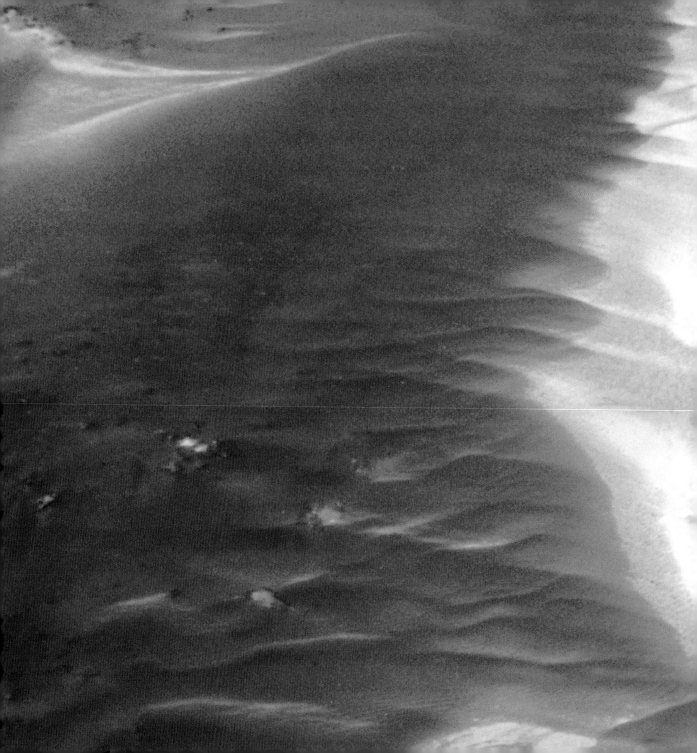

marketing

Australian pearls compete on the world market with similar pearls produced in Indonesia, Burma, Thailand and the Philippines. All these countries have lower labour costs than Australia, but this advantage is offset by the technology and expertise available in Australia.

Australian pearls are well regarded, frequently being of better quality, and worth higher prices, than pearls from other places. Demand for Australian pearls always exceeds supply. Like the diamond market, the pearl market has been run by a cartel, although now it is beginning to open up. Unlike

the market for diamonds or other cut stones, it has no firm criteria for setting pearl prices. A close knowledge of the market is essential: knowing what prices have recently been paid, how the world economy is faring and what the popular pearl characteristics are. Very few people are experts in pricing pearls.

The Japan Export Overseas Pearl Producers' Association is a cartel formed by the Japanese in 1964 as a way of avoiding competition between Japanese *Akoya* pearls and pearls from other

countries. The cartel set floor prices for pearls and stipulated that Japanese dealers bring all pearls produced overseas back to Japan for marketing and that no pearls under 10 millimetres in size be produced outside Japan. Until a few years ago the cartel still had a strong hold on the market: most Australian pearls went to Japan before being distributed to other parts of the world. The pearls were mostly sold unworked, or in temporary strands.

But times are changing. Most of the small Australian pearl farmers market their pearls through Rosario Autore, a Sydney-based pearl broker with a worldwide marketing network. He now sells less than half his product to Japan; the majority is sold directly to clients in the

USA, Italy, Germany, Hong Kong, Thailand and elsewhere. Typical buyers might be pearl wholesalers, manufacturing jewellers or large retail jewellers who visit Australia to view the pearls and make their choice. Paspaley

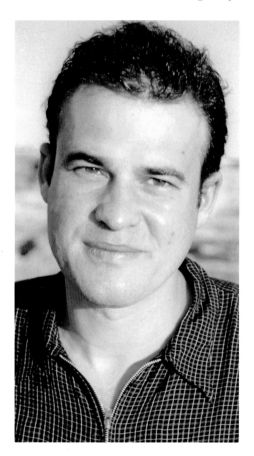

far left:
South Sea Pearls from Australia and Tahiti, Linneys of Broome & Subiaco collection

left: **Rosario Autore, a Sydney-based pearl broker**

103

Pearling Company, producer of more than half Australia's pearls, is also selling directly to international clients and has staged several pearl auctions. More emphasis is being placed on adding value to the pearls by matching them for strands and earrings, and by making them into jewellery.

The combined pearl production from all Australian pearl farms is in the vicinity of one tonne per year, with an export value of $200 million. About the same quantity of white South Sea pearls is produced in Indonesia, the Philippines and Burma. By comparison, the total production of black pearls (principally from Tahiti) is now about five tonnes annually; Japan produces 100 tonnes of the smaller *Akoya* pearls each year (down from a peak of more than 140 tonnes in 1966), while the production of freshwater pearls (mainly in China) has increased dramatically to several hundred tonnes each year.

below and right:
Australian South Sea Pearls

Linneys Broome & Subiaco

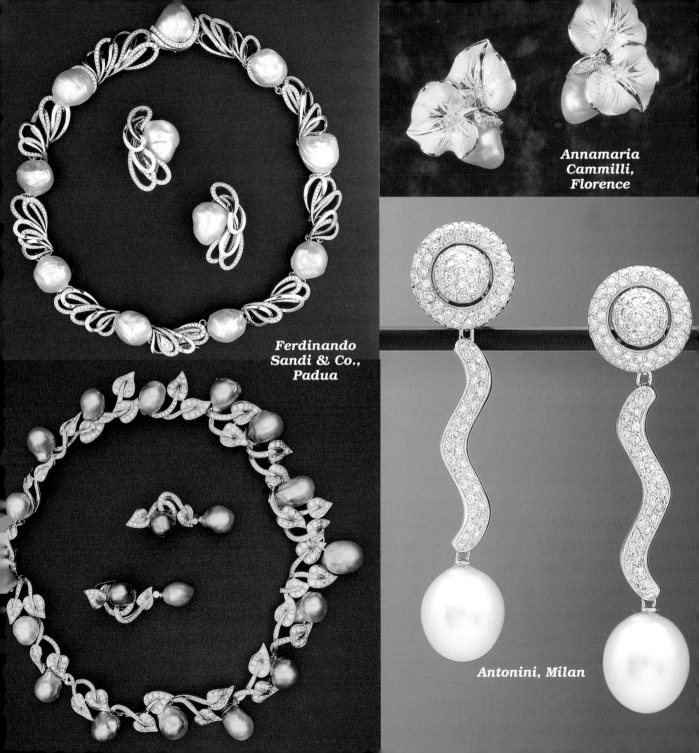

Annamaria Cammilli, Florence

Ferdinando Sandi & Co., Padua

Antonini, Milan

JOURNEY'S END

choosing a pearl. . .

The prospect of choosing pearls, whether loose or set into jewellery, may seem daunting to people who have never purchased them before. Several different types of pearls are available, grown in different species of oyster or by different processes. Each type has its own set of characteristics and price-tag, but the grading criteria discussed in Section 9 apply to them all. When buying pearls, it is important to remember that even though a pearl of one shape and colour might cost more than another, this does not necessarily mean that it is a pearl of better quality. Shape and colour are subjective factors.

Someone preferring a yellow baroque pearl, which might be less than a fifth the price of a silver-coloured round one, should not be put off by thinking that the lower price is a reflection of poorer quality. Prices are an indication of market demand as well as of quality and opportunities for bargains may therefore arise. But one should never compromise on lustre; good lustre is the most important characteristic of a gem quality pearl. Look for clarity of reflected images in the surface of the pearl: a mirror–like image is

a sign of good lustre. A sense of depth when looking into a pearl is also important, because it probably means there is a thick uniform coating of nacre over the nucleus.

Traditional pearl necklaces remain the classical way to present pearls, and more pearls are used for making necklaces than for any other type of jewellery. However pearls lend themselves to use in many other ways. When making a purchase it is often helpful to think about the way the pearl will be used, because this can influence the choice of shape and size. Unlike other gemstones, pearls cannot be cut. Thus the shape of the pearl tells the designer how it should be made up. Round pearls can easily be used in any jewellery, while the

pear-shaped drop pearls are more suitable for pendants and earrings; the flattened appearance of buttons for rings and brooches. Baroque pearls of irregular shape are frequently incorporated into innovative modern designs whose possibilities are limited only by the imagination. Smaller pearls are often preferred for rings because the pearl will not protrude too much, and for earrings because bigger sizes apply greater weight to the earlobes.

far left:
jewellery from the Linneys of Broome & Subiaco collection

left: **16th century Russian icon 'Madonna and Child'**

113

Here is an introduction to the types of pearls which are likely to be encountered:

Australian South Sea pearls, which are also called 'Broome pearls', are grown in the silver or gold-lipped pearl oyster, *Pinctada maxima*, and are considered by most experts to be the best pearls in the world. They account for almost all the pearls grown in Australia. They are also grown in Indonesia, Thailand, Burma and the Philippines. Worldwide, less than two tonnes of these pearls are produced each year, of which about half are grown in Australia. A full description of the pearl farming methods used to grow Australian South Sea pearls was given in Part 2.

selection of jewellery from Linneys of Broome & Subiaco

Australian South Sea pearls are usually white or silver coloured, but they can also come in shades of yellow or blue-grey. Iridescent overtones are mostly pink or green. Their sizes range from 10 to 20 millimetres, but pearls larger than 16 millimetres are rare.

Prices of Australian South Sea pearls vary from $100 for a 10 millimetre baroque to several tens of thousands for a perfect 17 millimetre round pearl. A necklace of moderate quality pearls might cost around $10,000, but a strand of good quality would cost several times more. Extremely rare strands of 13 to 16 millimetre diameter, spherical, silver-pink pearls of perfect quality can bear price tags of hundreds of thousands of dollars.

Black South Sea pearls, also called 'Tahitian pearls', are grown in the black-lipped pearl oyster, *Pinctada margaritifera*. This species is found in the atolls of Polynesia and other Pacific Islands. The culture of black pearls began in Tahiti less than thirty years ago; prior to that, the extremely rare natural black pearls were worth a king's ransom.

Because it is fairly simple to collect spat and rear pearl oysters in the Polynesian atolls, and because of the numerous protected atoll lagoons in the region, the pearl culturing process is far simpler and less costly for black pearls than it is for white pearls.

Black South Sea pearls are generally smaller than the white ones and range in size from 9 to 13 millimetres in diameter. A few black pearls reach 15 millimetres.

There is a great variety of colour in the pearls from black-lip oysters: peacock green is a famous and sought-after colour and the most valuable. Other colours include aubergine, purple, green, black, and shades from grey through cream to white.

Prices of black pearls are usually lower than for white South Sea pearls. Individual pearls of reasonable quality retail from $100 or so for a 9 millimetre diameter pearl to a few thousand dollars for one that is 12 or 13 millimetres in diameter and of gem quality.

Akoya, or Japanese pearls, are grown in the Japanese

pearl oyster, *Pinctada fucata martensii*. Most *akoya* pearls are still produced in Japan but now some are also grown, on an increasing scale, in China and India. The annual production of akoya pearls is huge – around 100 tonnes each year.

The *akoya* pearl oyster measures only six to nine centimetres across – less than half the size of Australia's silver–lipped pearl oyster. Smaller nuclei are implanted, so the resulting pearls

far left:
Very rare necklace of perfect Tahitian black pearls. Linneys of Broome & Subiaco collection

above:
Akoya oyster, Pinctada fucata martensii

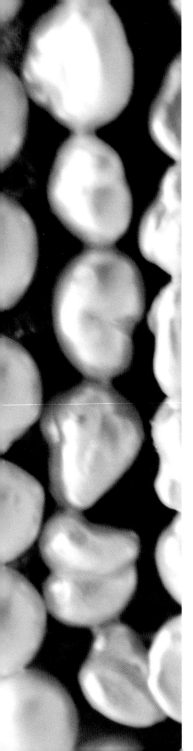

are smaller than Australian pearls, ranging from three to nine millimetres in diameter.

Akoya pearls are usually harvested earlier than Australian pearls, sometimes in as little as six to nine months. Such an early harvest means that the nacre is thinner – frequently less than half a millimetre thick, occasionally as little as 0.1 millimetre – and less likely to withstand normal wear and tear. Thin layers of nacre will abrade and chip off, exposing the nucleus. *Akoya* pearls are well suited to earrings and brooches which are subject to less wear and tear than other jewellery. There are some very good quality Japanese pearls with a one millimetre nacre coating, but these take at least four years to grow and are very expensive.

Almost all *akoya* pearls are chemically treated after harvest to enhance their colour and lustre. Unfortunately the treatments are not always stable, so the strand matched for colour today may not look as uniform in a few years time. The real advantage of *Akoya* pearls is their affordability. A necklace can be purchased for several hundred dollars, rather than the many thousands of dollars needed for a South Sea strand.

Keshi, or seed pearls, are described in the 'Harvest' section of Part 2. They appear identical to natural pearls, and are a by-product of pearl culture. The international term *keshi* means 'poppy seed' in Japanese, and is a reference to the small size of these pearls,

right:
**Mabe,
silver &
gold ring,
The Globe,
Broome**

which are seldom more than a few millimetres in diameter.

Keshi pearls are popular because they are made of solid nacre and usually have a bright lustre. Their irregular shape can be a stimulus and challenge to jewellery designers, and some of the most innovative jewellery is made using them.

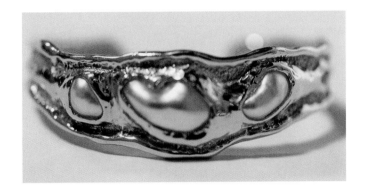

above:
**Keshi and gold
bangle, Linneys
of Broome &
Subiaco
collection**

Mabe pearls, as half or blister pearls are known in the jewellery trade, are made by glueing several hemispherical plastic beads to the inside of pearl oyster shells, as described in the 'Harvest' section of Part 2. *Mabe* is the Japanese name for the winged oyster, *Pteria penguin*, in which these pearls are commonly grown. They are also grown in silver lipped pearl oysters that have already grown round pearls.

The half pearls, about one millimetre thick, are drilled off the shell using a diamond-tipped hole saw and the nucleus is removed. The half pearl now resembles

half an empty egg shell. The inside is then scraped to remove any brown organic stain and sometimes it is painted to enhance colour and lustre. It is then filled with resin, backed with discs of mother-of-pearl, and the joined edges ground smooth. The resulting product is a *mabe* pearl.

Mabe pearls have thinner nacre than many other pearls and the mother-of-pearl disc that backs it is attached with glue. This mean that *mabe* pearls are not as robust as round pearls and should be treated with care to keep them from coming apart.

Mabe pearls are only a fraction the price of whole pearls. A pair of good quality *mabe*, processed and ready to set into jewellery, can be bought for $100 or so. The size of *mabe* pearls varies from 12 to 20 millimetres in diameter. Most are round in shape but drops, hearts, and ovals are also made.

bottom left:
silver and gold jewellery with mabe pearls, The Globe, Broome

Freshwater pearls are small, often irregularly shaped pearls that are grown in various species of freshwater mussel. They are made by introducing twenty or more tiny tissue grafts into the thick mantle of a live mussel. The results vary according to species, one of which produces crinkly-surfaced pearls of medium lustre that are about the size and shape of rice bubbles. Freshwater pearls generally have a lower proportion of organic material in their nacre than pearls from marine pearl oysters. This gives freshwater pearls a glassy lustre.

Several hundred tonnes of freshwater pearls are grown in China each year. They are the cheapest pearls available and can look attractive. A popular way to use them is in rope necklaces made of several strands twisted together.

Imitation pearls are marketed under many names such as 'Majorca pearls', 'shell-based pearl' and a host of brand names. They are glass or plastic beads, laquered or painted with a synthetic 'pearl essence' similar to nail polish, or dipped in a paste of fish scales and glue. They have never been inside a pearl oyster. The first imitation pearls were made last century in Spain and Portugal using an iridescent extract from sardine scales mixed with varnish.

A strand of imitation pearls retails for between twenty and one hundred dollars. For a buyer with a very limited budget, it may be more sensible to purchase a strand of good quality imitation pearls rather than a very poor quality strand of *akoya* pearls.

It is very simple to tell the difference between synthetic and real pearls. When scraped gently against the biting edge of the teeth, imitation pearls are smooth and waxy in texture, compared to the rough texture of real pearls caused by the overlapping layers of nacre. A cultured or natural pearl will also make a slight grating sound when drawn this way over the teeth.

Australian and Tahitian South Sea Pearls. Linneys of Broome & Subiaco collection.

...to cherish

Whatever pearls you own, their life will be extended if you follow a few simple practices that have regard for the chemical properties of calcium carbonate, from which pearls are made. Pearls can be damaged by acid. Perfume and perspiration are harmful to them. After each wearing it is advisable, especially in hot climates where people perspire more, to wipe pearls over with a damp cloth and then dry them before putting them away. Pearls are not brittle – if they have a thick coating they can withstand severe knocks – but they are relatively soft and can be damaged by abrasion. When worn

continuously in a way that puts them in constant contact with the skin, like a bracelet, they will soon begin to wear away. To protect them from abrasion, pearls should be stored apart from other jewellery and not kept with coins or chains in a jewellery pouch.

Pearl necklaces should be re-strung every few years, and the string knotted between each pearl. This will prevent the pearls sliding on the string and being damaged by friction. It also prevents the pearls from scattering in the event that the strand breaks.

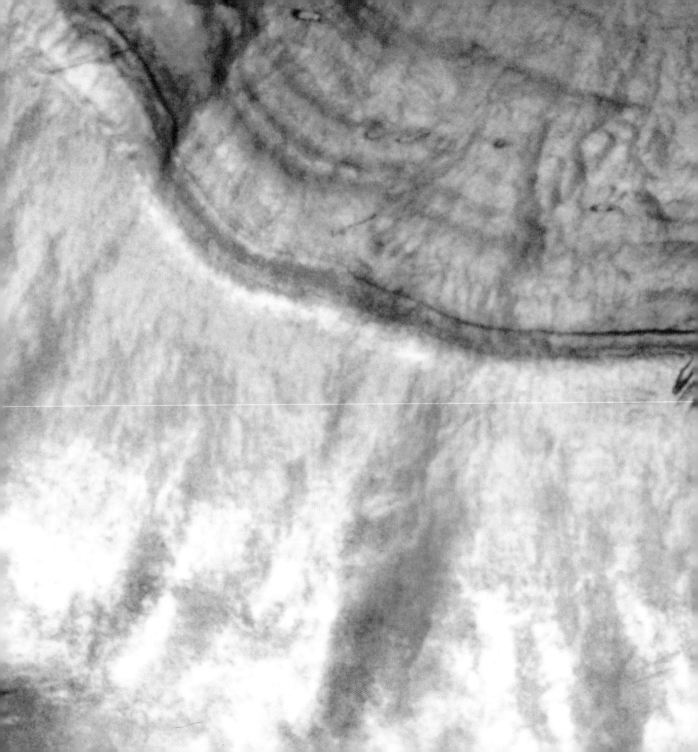

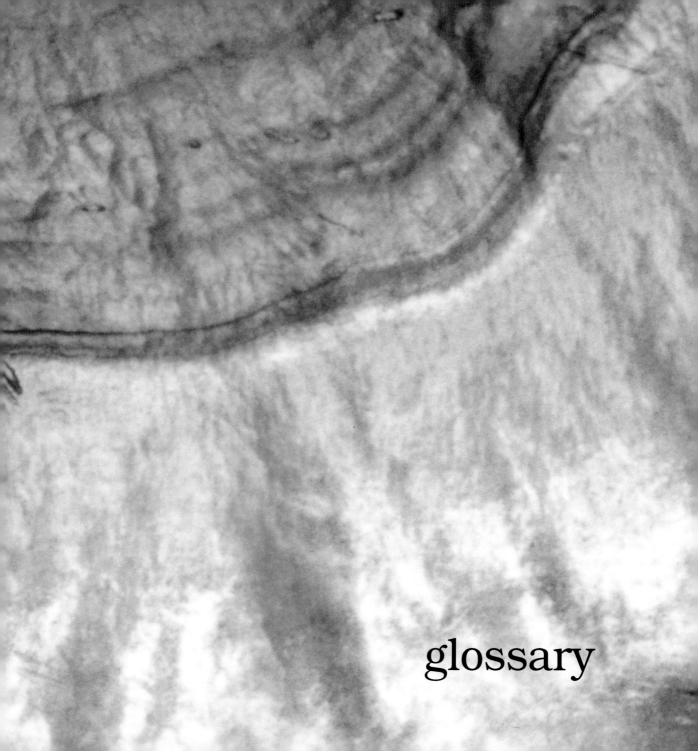

glossary

adductor muscle a large kidney-shaped muscle that controls the opening and closing of a pearl oyster shell. As **pearl shell meat** it is a by-product of pearl culture and is usually dried and sold to Asian markets.

***akoya* pearls** cultured pearls grown in the Japanese *akoya* pearl oyster, *Pinctada fucata martensi*.

big-bag a large net bag with a small parachute attached, used by divers to hold the pearl oysters they are collecting. Divers can inflate the parachute with air to assist their ascent.

black South Sea pearls cultured pearls grown in the black-lipped pearl oyster, *Pinctada margaritifera*.

booms the outriggers of a pearling boat to which the diving hoses are attached.

bottom the sea floor.

chicken shell young pearl oysters (see also **spat** and **shell**).

cultured pearl a pearl grown in a mollusc by inserting a piece of graft mantle tissue and, usually, a nucleus.

drift the passage of a dive boat, drifting with the tide, above a patch of oyster-bearing sea bottom.

dropper a rope, usually one centi-metre in diameter and a few metres long, used to hang panels of pearl oysters in the sea (compare **long-line**).

dump an area of sea bottom that is used as a temporary holding place for pearl oysters.

freshwater pearls cultured pearls grown in various species of freshwater mussels.

garden bottom a sea bed community of colourful sponges, coral, and seaweed in which pearl oysters often grow.

gonad the pearl oyster's reproductive organ, and the site where the nucleus and mantle graft are put when a pearl is seeded.

grading the process of grouping pearls by their characteristics of lustre, colour, size, shape, and flaws.

graft a small piece of mantle tissue, inserted during a pearl-seeding operation, which produces the pearl sac which in turn will produce the nacre coating around the nucleus.

grow-out the process of growing spat into mature pearl oysters.

half-pearls pearls made by gluing flat-based shapes to the inside of pearl shells. Also called *mabe*.

harvesting the operation to remove cultured pearls from pearl oysters, which can usually be done without killing the animal.

imitation pearls artificial pearls commonly made by coating glass or plastic beads with synthetic pearl paint.

keshi small pearls, without a nucleus, that occur inadvertently as a by-product of pearl culture.

longline a thick rope, buoyed by floats and anchored at each end, from which panels of pearl oysters are hung (compare **dropper**).

mabe the Japanese name for a species of pearl oyster called *Pteria penguin*, in which half-pearls are grown. Also a name for half-pearls (see half-pearls).

mantle a large, thin lobe of tissue that lies against the shell and secretes shell-forming substances. A piece of graft tissue used in the pearl-seeding operation is cut from the mantle.

micrometre (μm) one thousandth of a millimetre; also called micron.

mollusc a soft-bodied and usually hard-shelled animal of the phylum Mollusca, which includes all the pearl-producing animals.

momme 3.75 grams: the traditional Japanese weight measure for pearls.

mother-of-pearl the nacreous part of a shell (see **nacre**).

nacre the lustrous layered coating of the inside of pearl oyster shells and the outside of pearls. It is composed of calcium carbonate crystals in a matrix of protein and carbohydrate. The term mother-of-pearl is often used instead of nacre.

natural pearl a pearl formed by completely natural processes.

neaps the period of a tidal cycle with the least movement between low and high tides, during which diving for pearl oysters takes place. In the pearling industry each diving trip is usually called a neap.

neck-bag a net bag which is hung around a pearl-diver's neck and used to hold pearl oysters as they are collected.

nucleus the polished shell bead that is implanted during a seeding operation, around which nacre forms to make a cultured pearl.

patch an area of sea bottom on which pearl oysters are growing.

pearl shell meat the dried or frozen adductor muscle of pearl oysters which is sold as a by-product of pearl culture, and which is sometimes said to be an aphrodisiac (see **adductor muscle**).

pearl sac the nacre-secreting cells enclosing a forming pearl.

pearl oyster the common name for pearl producing molluscs, especially those of the genus *Pinctada* which are most important for commercial pearl production.

Pinctada maxima the scientific name of the silver-lipped pearl oyster, which is the largest of the pearl oysters, and upon which the Australian pearling industry is based.

potato country a type of sandy sea bed that is scattered with sea-squirts, and on which pearl oysters grow.

quota the number of pearl oysters, set by the Fisheries Department, that a pearling company may catch in any year.

round pearl a cultured pearl which is made using a spherical nucleus, surgically inserted into the body of a pearl oyster. The resulting pearl is not always round — it may be baroque or shaped like a drop, oval or button (see **nucleus** and **graft**).

seeding the operation of inserting a bead nucleus and piece of mantle graft into a pearl oyster, that results in a cultured pearl.

shell live pearl oysters.

spat juvenile pearl oysters, especially just after development from larvae.

spat collection the collection of wild spat onto artificial materials hung in the sea.

springs the period of tide with the greatest difference between high and low levels. Tidal currents during springs are usually too severe for divers to collect shell.

technician the person who performs operations, such as **seeding** and **harvesting**, on pearl oysters.

turning program a schedule for turning pearl oysters from side to side after the seeding operation to help the **pearl sac** form evenly. It may last a month or more.

Australian South Sea pearls cultured pearls grown in the silver or gold-lipped pearl oyster, *Pinctada maxima*.

Further reading

Books

Bain, M.A. *Full Fathom Five*. Artlook Books, Perth, 1982. A well referenced historical account of the Australian mother-of-pearl industry.

Doubilet, David: *Pearls: from the myths to modern pearl culture*. Schoeffel Pearl Culture, Stuttgart, 1996.

Farn, A.E. *Pearls: Natural, Cultured and Imitation*. Butterworths, London, 1986. Good explanations of pearl testing techniques.

Joyce, K. and S. Addison. *Pearls: Ornament & Obsession*. Thames and Hudson, London, 1992. A lavishly illustrated book showing the place of pearls in myth, history, and the Arts.

Kunz, G.F. and C.H. Stevenson. *The Book of the Pearl*. Century Co., New York, 1908. A classic work that gives a complete description of the pearling industry world-wide, before the time of cultured pearls.

Mazloum, Claude: *Jewellery Gem by Gem*, Gremese International, 1996.

Reed, William: *Pearl Oysters of Polynesia*. Societe des Oceanistes, 1973

Salomon, Pauli and Roudnitska: *La Magique de la Perle Noire*. Tahiti Perles, 1986.

Taburiaux, Jean: *La perle et ses secrets*, 1986.

Ward, F. *Pearls*. Gem Book Publishers, Bethesda, USA, 1995. A small, well-illustrated book about different types of pearls.

Reports

Dybdahl, R. and D.A. Pass. *An Investigation of Mortality of the Pearl Oyster, Pinctada maxima, in Western Australia*. Report No. 71, Fisheries Department of W.A., Perth, 1986.

Malone, F.J., D.A. Hancock and B. Jeffriess. *Final Report of the Pearling Industry Review Committee*. Fisheries Management Paper No. 17, Fisheries Dept. of W.A., Perth, 1988.

Other

Pamplets produced by the Fisheries Department of Western Australia and the Departments of Primary Industry and Fisheries in the Northern Territory and Queensland. Quota information given in this book was sourced from these Departments.